On Cleaving to God

attributed to
Saint Albert The Great

a lamp post book

ON CLEAVING TO GOD
Attributed to Saint Albert the Great

Layout and Design Copyright © 2008 by Lamp Post Inc.
Additional Content Copyright © 2008 by Lamp Post Inc.
All rights reserved.

Print ISBN 10: 1-60039-107-9
Print ISBN 13: 978-1-60039-107-1

ebook ISBN 10: 1-60039-709-3
ebook ISBN 13: 978-1-60039-709-7

Published by Lamp Post Inc.

Without limiting the rights under copyright reserved above, no part of this publication — whether in printed or ebook format, or any other published derivation — may be reproduced, stored in or introduced into a retrieval system, or transmitted, in any form or by any means (electronic, mechanical, photocopying, recording or otherwise), without the prior written permission of the publisher.

The scanning, uploading, and distribution of this book via the Internet or via any other means without the permission of the publisher is illegal and punishable by law. Please purchase only authorized electronic editions and do not participate in or encourage electronic piracy of copyrightable materials.

Lamp Post Inc. assumes no responsibility for any errors or inaccuracies that may appear in this book.

www.lamppostpubs.com

ALBERT THE GREAT

or Albertus Magnus, Medieval theologian, philosopher, and scientist
b. 1193 or 1206, d. 1280

A nobleman of Bollstådt in Swabia, he joined the Dominicans (in 1223) and taught at Hildesheim, Freiburg, Regensburg, Strasbourg, and Cologne before the Univ. of Paris made him doctor of theology in 1245. Later he taught again at Cologne, and he was also briefly (1260-62) bishop of Regensburg. He was a thorough student of Aristotle, and he not only followed Robert Grosseteste in his approach to Aristotelian thought but also did much to introduce Aristotle's scientific treatises and scientific method to Europe. Like Roger Bacon, he had a scientific interest in nature. He made notable botanical observations (recorded in such works as De vegetabilibus), was the first to produce arsenic in a free form, and studied the combinations of metals. In philosophy he set out in his Summa theologiae to controvert Averroäs and others and to reconcile the apparent contradictions of Aristotelianism and Christian thought. He wrote many treatises, and many more have been ascribed to him; the problem of determining which are genuinely of his authorship is difficult. He was a strong influence on his favorite pupil, St. Thomas Aquinas. Albertus was canonized in 1931. Feast: Nov. 15.

Translator's Introduction

This famous and much loved little treatise, On Cleaving to God, (*De Adhaerendo Deo*) has always been attributed to Saint Albert the Great, who lived from about 1200 to 1280, and was one of the most respected theologians of his time. He was moreover a voluminous writer in the scholastic tradition, and, amongst other things, Bishop of Ratisbonne and one of the teachers of Eckhart at Paris University. The Latin text of which this is a translation is found in volume 37 of his Opera Omnia published in Paris in 1898.

However almost all modern scholars are agreed that the work could not have been written by him, at least certainly not in its present form. It contains many implicit references and quotations from writers who lived well after Albert the Great. It is quite clear from the opening words of the treatise that it is in essence the private anthology of a contemplative or would-be contemplative, culled from many different sources, and including thoughts of his own. From the references included, it would seem to belong, at least in its present form to an unknown writer of the fifteenth century.

However, it has often been pointed out that the first nine chapters seem to be of a somewhat different character to the remaining seven. Indeed most of the directly contemplative and mystical material in the work is contained in this first half, while the second section is concerned largely with more general matters of ordinary Christian piety. It has therefore been suggested that it is perhaps possible that a later hand has to some extent reworked and extended an original, shorter text, that could perhaps even go back to Albert the Great. Albert, we know, wrote a commentary on the teachings of the famous St. Dionysius, and this work, particularly in the first nine chapters is full of "Dionysian" themes. This could indicate that these chapters at least may belong to Albert the Great, or, alternatively, it could explain how it came to be attributed to him. The fact remains, whichever way round, that the work stands on its own merits as a classic of Western contemplative mysticism in the *Via Negativa* tradition. It has indeed been frequently called a supplement to the Imitation of Christ.

In view of all these considerations, and in view of the fact that the work has always been attributed to Albert the Great (and all libraries and catalogues include it under his name), I have felt it best to leave it attached to his name, though with the above reservations. After all, Anonymous has dozens of works attributed to him that were actually written by someone else, so perhaps for once it is only fair to attribute an anonymous work to an actual person. Anyone who has ever tried to look for a work by Anonymous in a big library catalogue will, I feel confident, be grateful to me!

Like Anonymous, I lay no claims to copyright on this translation. I commit it, and a copy of the Latin original, to the deep in sure and certain hope that it will do its own work.

John Richards

jhr@universalist.worldonline.co.uk

ONE

ON THE HIGHEST AND SUPREME PERFECTION OF MAN, IN SO FAR AS IT IS POSSIBLE IN THIS LIFE

I have had the idea of writing something for myself on and about the state of complete and full abstraction from everything and of cleaving freely, confidently, nakedly and firmly to God alone, so as to describe it fully (in so far as it is possible in this abode of exile and pilgrimage), especially since the goal of Christian perfection is the love by which we cleave to God. In fact everyone is obligated, to this loving cleaving to God as necessary for salvation, in the form of observing the commandments and conforming to the divine will, and the observation of the commandments excludes everything that is contrary to the nature and habit of love, including mortal sin. Members of religious orders have committed themselves in addition to evangelical perfection, and to the things that constitute a voluntary and counselled perfection by means of which one may arrive more quickly to the supreme goal which is God. The observation of these additional commitments excludes as well the things that hinder the working and fervour of love, and without which one can come to God, and these include the renunciation of all things, of both body and mind, exactly as one's vow of profession entails. Since indeed the Lord God is Spirit, and those who worship him must worship in spirit and in truth, in other words, by knowledge and love, that is, understanding and desire, stripped of all images. This is what is referred to in Matthew 6.6, 'When you pray, enter into your inner chamber,' that is, your inner heart, 'and having closed the door,' that is of your senses, and there with a pure heart and a clear conscience, and with faith unfeigned, 'pray to your Father,' in spirit and in truth, 'in secret.' This can be done best when a man is disengaged and removed from everything else, and completely recollected within himself. There, in the presence of Jesus Christ, with everything, in general and individually, excluded and wiped out, the mind alone turns in security confidently to the Lord its God with its desire. In this way it pours itself forth into him in full sincerity with its whole heart and the yearning of its love, in the most inward part of all its faculties, and is plunged, enlarged, set on fire and dissolved into him.

Two

HOW ONE CAN CLING TO AND SEEK CHRIST ALONE, DISDAINING EVERYTHING ELSE

Certainly, anyone who desires and aims to arrive at and remain in such a state must needs above all have eyes and senses closed and not be inwardly involved or worried about anything, nor concerned or occupied with anything, but should completely reject all such things as irrelevant, harmful and dangerous. Then he should withdraw himself totally within himself and not pay any attention to any object entering the mind except Jesus Christ, the wounded one, alone, and so he should turn his attention with care and determination *through* him *into* him - that is, though the man into God, through the wounds of his humanity into the inmost reality of his divinity. Here he can commit himself and all that he has, individually and as a whole, promptly, securely and without discussion, to God's unwearying providence, in accordance with the words of Peter, *cast all your care upon him* (1 Peter 5.7), who can do everything. And again, *In nothing be anxious* (Philippians 4.6), or what is more, *Cast your burden upon the Lord, and he will sustain you.* (Psalm 55.22) Or again, *It is good for me to hold fast to God,* (Ps. 73.28) and *I have always set up God before me.* (Psalm 16.8) The bride too in the Song of Songs says, *I have found him whom my soul loves,* (Canticle 3.4) and again, *All good things came to me along with her.* (Wisdom 7.11) This, after all, is the hidden heavenly treasure, none other than the pearl of great price, which must be sought with resolution, esteeming it in humble faithfulness, eager diligence, and calm silence before all things, and preferring it even above physical comfort, or honour and renown. For what good does it do a religious if he gains the whole world but suffers the loss of his soul? Or what is the benefit of his state of life, the holiness of his profession, the virtue of his habit and tonsure, or the outer circumstances of his way of life if he is without a life of spiritual humility and truth in which Christ abides through a faith created by love. This is what Luke means by, *the Kingdom of God* (that is, Jesus Christ) *is within you.* (Luke 17.21)

Three

WHAT THE PERFECTION OF MAN CONSIST OF IN THIS LIFE

Now the more the mind is concerned about thinking and dealing with what is merely lower and human, the more it is separated from the experience in the intimacy of devotion of what is higher and heavenly, while the more fervently the memory, desire and intellect is withdrawn from what is below to what is above, the more perfect will be our prayer, and the purer our contemplation, since the two directions of our interest cannot both be perfect at the same time, being as different as light and darkness. He who cleaves to God is indeed translated into the light, while he who clings to the world is in the dark. So the supreme perfection of man in this life is to be so united to God that all his soul with all its faculties and powers are so gathered into the Lord God that he becomes one spirit with him, and remembers nothing except God, is aware of and recognises nothing but God, but with all his desires unified by the joy of love, he rests contentedly in the enjoyment of his Maker alone. Now the image of God as found in the soul consists of these three faculties, namely reason, memory and will, and so long as they are not completely stamped with God, the soul is not yet deiform in accordance with the initial creation of the soul. For the true pattern of the soul is God, with whom it must be imprinted, like wax with a seal, and carry the mark of his impress. But this can never be complete until the intellect is perfectly illuminated, according to its capacity, with the knowledge of God, who is perfect truth, until the will is perfectly focused on the love of the perfect good, and until the memory is fully absorbed in turning to and enjoying eternal happiness, and in gladly and contentedly resting in it. And since the glory of the beatitude which is achieved in our heavenly homeland consists in the complete fulfilment of these three faculties, it follows that perfect initiation of them is perfection in this life.

FOUR

HOW MAN'S ACTIVITY SHOULD BE PURELY IN THE INTELLECT AND NOT IN THE SENSES

Happy therefore is the person who by continual removal of fantasies and images, by turning within, and raising the mind to God, finally manages to dispense with the products of the imagination, and by so doing works within, nakedly and simply, and with a pure understanding and will, on the the simplest of all objects, God. So eliminate from your mind all fantasies, objects, images and shapes of all things other than God, so that, with just naked understanding, intent and will, your practice will be concerned with God himself within you. For this is the end of all spiritual exercises - to turn the mind to the Lord God and rest in him with a completely pure understanding and a completely devoted will, without the entanglements and fantasies of the imagination. This sort of exercise is not practised by fleshly organs nor by the exterior senses, but by that by which one is indeed a man. For a man is precisely understanding and will. For that reason, in so far as a man is still playing with the products of the imagination and the senses, and holds to them, it is obvious that he has not yet emerged from the motivation and limitations of his animal nature, that is of that which he shares in common with the animals. For these know and feel objects by means of recognised shapes and sense impressions and no more, since they do not possess the higher powers of the soul. But it is different with man, who is created in the image and likeness of God with understanding, will, and free choice, through which he should be directly, purely and nakedly impressed and united with God, and firmly adhere to him. For this reason the Devil tries eagerly and with all his power to hinder this practice so far as he can, being envious of this in man, since it is a sort of prelude and initiation of eternal life. So he is always trying to draw man's mind away from the Lord God, now by temptations or passions, now by superfluous worries and pointless cares, now by restlessness and distracting conversation and senseless curiosity, now by the study of subtle books, irrelevant discussion, gossip and news, now by hardships, now by opposition, etc. Such matters may seem trivial enough and hardly sinful, but they are a great hindrance to this holy exercise and practice. Therefore, even if they may appear useful and necessary, they should be rejected, whether great or small, as harmful and dangerous, and put out of our minds. Above all therefore it is necessary that things heard, seen, done and said, and other such things, must be received without adding things from the imagination, without mental associations and without emotional involvement, and one should not let past or future associations, implications or constructs of the imagination form and grow. For when constructs of the imagination are not allowed to enter the memory and mind, a man is not hindered, whether he be engaged in prayer, meditation, or reciting psalms, or in any other practice or spiritual exercise, nor will they recur again. So commit yourself confidently and without hesitation, all that you are, and everything else, individually and in general, to the unfailing and totally reliable providence of God, in silence and in peace, and he will fight for you. He will liberate you and comfort you more fully, more effectively and more satisfactorily than if you were to dream about it all the time, day and night, and were to cast around frantically all over the place with the futile and confused thoughts of your mind in bondage, nor will you wear out your mind and body, wasting your time, and stupidly and pointlessly exhausting your strength. So accept everything, separately and in general, wherever it comes from and whatever its origin, in silence and peace, and with an equal mind, as coming to you from a father's hand and his divine providence. So render your imagination bare of the images of all physical things as is appropriate to your state and profession, so that you can cling to him with a bare and undivided mind, as you have so often and so completely vowed to do, without anything whatever being able to come between your soul and him, so that you can pass purely and unwaveringly from the wounds of his humanity into the light of his divinity.

FIVE

ON PURITY OF HEART WHICH IS TO BE SOUGHT ABOVE ALL THINGS

If your desire and aim is to reach the destination of the path and home of true happiness, of grace and glory, by a straight and safe way then earnestly apply your mind to seek constant purity of heart, clarity of mind and calm of the senses. Gather up your heart's desire and fix it continually on the Lord God above. To do so you must withdraw yourself so far as you can from friends and from everyone else, and from the activities that hinder you from such a purpose. Grasp every opportunity when you can find the place, time and means to devote yourself to silence and contemplation, and gathering the secret fruits of silence, so that you can escape the shipwreck of this present age and avoid the restless agitation of the noisy world. For this reason apply yourself at all times to purity, clarity and peace of heart above all things, so that, so far as possible, you can keep the doors of your heart resolutely barred to the forms and images of the physical senses and worldly imaginations by shutting off the doors of the physical senses and turning within yourself. After all, purity of heart is recognised as the most important thing among all spiritual practices, as its final aim, and the reward for all the labours that a spiritual-minded person and true religious may undertake in this life. For this reason you should with all care, intelligence and effort free your heart, senses and desires from everything that can hinder their liberty, and above all from everything in the world that could possibly bind and overcome you. So struggle in this way to draw together all the distractions of your heart and desires of your mind into one true, simple and supreme good, to keep them gathered within yourself in one place, and by this means to remain always joined to things divine and to God in your mind, to abandon the unreliable things of earth, and be able to translate your mind continually to the things above within yourself in Jesus Christ. To which end, if you have begun to strip and purify yourself of images and imaginations and to simplify and still your heart and mind in the Lord God so that you can draw and taste the well of divine grace in everything within yourself, and so that you are united to God in your mind by a good will, then this itself is enough for you in place of all study and reading of holy scripture, and as demonstration of love of God and neighbour, as devotion itself testifies. So simplify your heart with all care, diligence and effort so that still and at peace from the products of the imagination you can turn round and remain always in the Lord within yourself, as if your mind were already in the now of eternity, that is of the godhead. In this way you will be able to renounce yourself through love of Jesus Christ, with a pure heart, clean conscience and unfeigned faith, and commit yourself completely and fully to God in all difficulties and eventualities, and be willing to submit yourself patiently to his will and good pleasure at all times. For this to come about you must repeatedly retreat into your heart and remain there, keeping yourself free from everything, so far as is possible. You must always keep the eye of your mind clear and still. You must guard your understanding from daydreams and thoughts of earthly things. You must completely free the inclination of your will from worldly cares and cling with all your being to the supreme true good with fervent love. You must keep your memory always lifted up and firmly anchored in that same true supreme good and only uncreated reality. In just this way your whole mind gathered up with all its powers and faculties in God, may become one spirit with him, in whom the supreme perfection of life is known to consist. This is the true union of spirit and love by which a man is made compliant to all the impulses of the supreme and eternal will, so that he becomes by grace what God is by nature. At the same time it should be noted that in the very moment in which one is able, by God's help, to overcome one's own will, that is to cast away from oneself inordinate love or strong feeling, in other words so as to dare simply to trust God completely in all one's needs, by this very fact one becomes so pleasing to God that his grace is imparted to one, and through that very grace one experiences that true love and devotion which drives out all uncertainty and fear and has full confidence in God. What is more, there can be no greater happiness than to place one's all in him who lacks nothing. So why do you still remain in yourself where you cannot stay. Cast yourself, all of yourself, with confidence into God and he will sustain you, heal you and make you safe. If you dwell on these things faithfully within, they will do more to confer a happy life on you than all riches, pleasures and honours, and above all the wisdom and knowledge of this present deceitful world and its life, even if you were to excel in them all that ever lived.

SIX

THAT THE DEVOUT MAN SHOULD CLEAVE TO GOD WITH NAKED UNDERSTANDING AND WILL

The more you strip yourself of the products of the imagination and involvement in external, worldly things and the objects of the senses, the more your soul will recover its strength and its inner senses so that it can appreciate the things which are above. So learn to withdraw from imaginations and the images of physical things, since what pleases God above everything is a mind bare of those sorts of forms and objects, for it is his delight to be with the sons of men, that is those who, at peace from such activities, distractions and passions, seek him with a pure and simple mind, empty themselves for him, and cleave to him. Otherwise, if your memory, imagination and thought is often involved with such things, you must needs be filled with the thought of new things or memories of old ones, or identified with other changing objects. As a result, the Holy Spirit withholds itself from thoughts bereft of understanding. So the true lover of Jesus Christ should be so united through good will in his understanding with the divine will and goodness, and be so bare of all imaginations and passions that he does not even notice whether he is being mocked or loved, or something is being done to him. For a good will turns everything to good and is above everything. So if the will is good and is obedient and united to God with pure understanding, he is not hurt even if the flesh and the senses and the outer man is moved to evil, and is slow to good, or even if the inner man is slow to feel devotion, but should simply cleave to God with faith and good will in naked understanding. He is doing this if he is conscious of all his own imperfection and nothingness, recognises his good to consist in his Creator alone, abandons himself with all his faculties and powers, and all creatures, and immerses himself wholly and completely in the Creator, so that he directs all his actions purely and entirely in his Lord God, and seeks nothing apart from him, in whom he recognises all good and all joy of perfection to be found. And he is so transformed in a certain sense into God that he cannot think, understand, love or remember anything but God himself and the things of God. Other creatures however and even himself he does not see, except in God, nor does he love anything except God alone, nor remember anything about them or himself except in God. This knowledge of the truth always makes the soul humble, ready to judge itself and not others, while on the contrary worldly wisdom makes the soul proud, futile, inflated and puffed up with wind. So let this be the fundamental spiritual doctrine leading to the knowledge of God, his service and familiarity with him, that if you want to truly possess God, you must strip your heart of all love of things of the senses, not just of certain creatures, so that you can turn to the Lord your God with a simple and whole heart and with all your power, freely and without any double-mindedness, care or anxiety, but with full confidence in his providence alone about everything.

SEVEN

HOW THE HEART SHOULD BE GATHERED WITHIN ITSELF

What is more, as is said in the book On the Spirit and the Soul (of St. Augustine), to ascend to God means to enter into oneself. He who entering within and penetrating his inmost nature, goes beyond himself, he is truly ascending to God. So let us withdraw our hearts from the distractions of this world, and recall them to the inner joys, so that we can establish them to some degree in the light of divine contemplation. For this is the life and peace of our hearts - to be established by intent in the love of God, and to be sweetly remade by his comforting. But the reason why we are in so many ways hindered in the practical enjoyment of this matter and are unable to get into it is clearly because the human mind is so distracted by worries that it cannot bring its memory to turn within, is so clouded by its imaginations that it cannot return to itself with its understanding, and is so drawn away by its desires that it is quite unable to come back to itself by desire for inner sweetness and spiritual joy. Thus it is so prostrate among the sense objects presented to it that it cannot enter into itself as the image of God. It is therefore right and necessary for the mind to raise itself above itself and everything created by the abandonment of everything, with humble reverence and great trust, and to say within itself, He whom I seek, love, thirst for and desire from everything and more than anything is not a thing of the senses or the imagination, but is above everything that can be experienced by the senses and the intellect. He cannot be experienced by any of the senses, but is completely desirable to my will. He is moreover not discernable, but is perfectly desirable to my inner affections. He cannot be comprehended, but can be loved in his fullness with a pure heart, for he is above all lovable and desirable, and of infinite goodness and perfection. And then a darkness comes over the mind and it is raised up into itself and penetrates even deeper. And the more inward-looking the desire for it, the more powerful this means of ascent to the mysterious contemplation of the holy Trinity in Unity and Unity in Trinity in Jesus Christ is, and the more interior the yearning, the more productive it is. Certainly in matters spiritual the more inward they are the greater they are as spiritual experiences. For this reason, never give up, never stop until you have tasted some pledge, as I might say, or foretaste of the future full experience, and until you have obtained the satisfaction of however small a first fruits of the divine joy. And do not give up pursuing it and following its scent until you have seen the God of gods in Sion. Do not stop or turn back in your spiritual journey and your union and adherence to God within you until you have achieved what you have been seeking. Take as a pattern of this the example of those climbing an ordinary mountain. If our mind is involved by its desires in the things which are going on below, it is immediately carried away by endless distractions and side tracks, and being to some extent divided against itself, is weakened and as it were scattered amongst the things which it seeks with its desires. The result is ceaseless movement, travel without an arrival, and labour without rest. If on the other hand our heart and mind can withdraw itself by its desire and love from the infinite distraction below of the things beneath it, can learn to be with itself, abandoning these lower things and gathering itself within itself into the one unchanging and satisfying good, and can hold to it inseparably with its will, it is correspondingly more and more gathered together in one and strengthened, as it is raised up by knowledge and desire. In this way it will become accustomed to the true supreme good within itself until it will be made completely immovable and arrive securely at that true life which is the Lord God himself, so that it can now rest in him within and in peace without any changeability or vicissitude of time, perfectly gathered within itself in the secret divine abode in Christ Jesus who is the way for those who come to him, the truth and life.

EIGHT

HOW A RELIGIOUS MAN SHOULD COMMIT HIMSELF TO GOD IN ALL CIRCUMSTANCES WHATSOEVER

I am now completely convinced that you will recognise from these arguments that the more you strip yourself of the products of your imagination and all worldly and created things, and are united to God with your intellect by a good will, the closer you will approach the state of innocence and perfection. What could be better? And what could be more happy and joyful? Above all it is important for you to keep your mind bare - without imaginations and images and free of any sort of entanglement, so that you are not concerned about either the world, friends, prosperity or adversity, or anything present, past or future, whether in yourself or in others - not even your own sins. But consider yourself with a certain pure simplicity to be alone with God outside the world, and as if your mind were already in eternity and separated from the body so that it will certainly not bother about worldly things or be concerned about the state of the world, about peace or war, about good weather or rain, or about anything at all in this world, but with complete docility will turn to God alone, be empty for him and cleave to him. So now in this way ignore your body and all created things, present or future, and direct the high point of your mind and spirit directly, as best you can, naked and unencumbered on the uncreated light. And let your spirit be cleansed in this way from all imaginations, coverings and things obscuring its vision, like an angel (not) tied to a body, who is not hindered by the works of the flesh nor tangled in vain and wandering thoughts. Let your spirit therefore arm itself against all temptations, vexations, and injuries so that it can persevere steadily in God when attacked by either face of fortune. So that when some inner disturbance or boredom or mental confusion come you will not be indignant or dejected because of it, nor run back to vocal prayers or other forms of consolation, but only to lift yourself up in your intellect by a good will to hold on to God with your mind whether the natural inclination of the body wills it or not. The religious-minded soul should be so united to God and should have or render its will so conformed to the divine will that it is not occupied with any created thing or cling to it any more than before it was created, and as if nothing existed except God and the soul itself. And in this way it should accept everything confidently and equally, in general and in particular, from the hand of divine providence, agreeing in everything with the Lord in patience, peace and silence. The thing is that the most important thing of all for a spiritual life is to strip the mind of all imaginations so that one can be united in one's intellect to God by a good will, and conformed to him. Besides, nothing will then be intermediary between you and God. This is obvious, since nothing external will stand between you when by the vow of voluntary poverty you will have removed the possession of anything whatsoever, and by the vow of chastity you will have abandoned your body, and by obedience you will have given up your will and your soul itself. And in this way nothing will be left to stand between you and God. That you are a religious person is indicated by your profession, your state, and now your habit and tonsure and such like, but whether you are only a religious in appearance or a real one, you will find out. Bear in mind therefore how greatly you have fallen away and sin against the Lord your God and all his justice if you behave otherwise and cling with your will and love to what is created rather than to the Creator himself, putting the created before the Creator.

NINE

HOW MUCH THE CONTEMPLATION OF GOD IS TO BE PREFERRED TO ALL OTHER EXERCISES

Now since all things other than God are the effect and work of the Creator himself, their having ability and being is a limited power and existence, and being as they are created out of nothing, they are circumscribed by the effects of their nothingness, while their tendency of themselves towards nothingness means that we receive our existence, preservation and activity moment by moment from the Creator himself, along with whatever other qualities created things may have, just as we receive their insufficiency to any action of themselves, both with regard to themselves and to others, in relation to him whose operation they are, they remain as a nothing before something which exists, and as something finite before what is infinite. For this reason let all our actual contemplation, life and activity take place in him alone, about him, for him and towards him who is able and capable to produce with a single nod of his will things infinitely more perfect than any that exist now. No contemplation and fruition of love, whether intellectual or affective, is more useful, more perfect and more satisfying than that which is of God himself, the Creator, our supreme and true Good, from whom, through whom and to whom are all things. He is infinitely satisfying both to himself and to all others, who contains within himself in absolute simplicity and from all eternity the perfection of all things, in whom there is nothing which is not himself, before whom and through whom remain the causes of all things impermanent, and in whom dwell the unchanging origins of all changing things, while even the eternal reasons of all temporal things, rational and irrational, abide in him. He brings everything to completion, and fills all things, in general and in particular, completely and essentially with himself. He is more intimately and more really present to everything by his being than each thing is to itself, for in him all things are united together, and live in him eternally. What is more, if someone, out of weakness or from lack of intellectual practice, is detained longer in the contemplation of created things, this supreme, true and fruitful contemplation may still be seen as possible for mortal man, so that there may take place an upward leap in all his contemplations and meditations, whether about created things or the Creator, and the appreciation of God the Creator himself, the One and Three, may surge up within so that he come to burn with the fire of divine love and the true life in himself and in others, in such a way as to make him deserving of the joy of eternal life. Even in this one should bear in mind the difference between the contemplation of faithful Catholics and that of pagan philosophers, for the contemplation of the philosophers is for the perfection of the contemplator himself, and consequently it is confined to the intellect and their aim in it is intellectual knowledge. But the contemplation of the Saints, and of Catholics, is for the love of him, that is of the God they are contemplating. As a result it is not confined in the final analysis to the intellect in knowledge, but crosses over into the will through love. That is why the Saints in their contemplation have the love of God as their principal aim, since it is more satisfying to know and possess even the Lord Jesus Christ spiritually through grace than physically or even really but without grace. Furthermore, while the soul is withdrawn from everything and is turned within, the eye of contemplation is opened and sets itself up a ladder by which it can pass to the contemplation of God. By this contemplation the soul is set on fire for eternal things by the heavenly and divine good things it experiences, and views all the things of time from a distance and as if they were nothing. Hence when we approach God by the way of negation, we first deny him everything that can be experienced by the body, the senses and the imagination, secondly even things experienceable by the intellect, and finally even being itself in so far as it is found in created things. This, so far as the nature of the way is concerned, is the best means of union with God, according to Dionysius. And this is the cloud in which God is said to dwell, which Moses entered, and through this came to the inaccessible light. Certainly, *it is not the spiritual which comes first, but the natural,* (1 Corinthians 15.46) so one must proceed by the usual order of things, from active work to the quiet of contemplation, and from moral virtues to spiritual and contemplative realities. Finally, my soul, why are you uselessly preoccupied with so many things, and always busy with them? Seek out and love the one supreme good, in which is all that is worth seeking, and that will be enough for you. Unhappy therefore is he who knows and possesses everything other than this, and does not know this. While if he knows everything as well as this, it is not from knowing them that he is better off but because of This. That is why John says, *This is eternal life, to know Thee,* etc. (John 17.3) and the prophet says, *I will be satisfied when your glory becomes manifest.* (Psalm 17.15)

Ten

THAT ONE SHOULD NOT BE CONCERNED ABOUT FEELING TANGIBLE DEVOTION SO MUCH AS ABOUT CLEAVING TO GOD WITH ONE'S WILL

Furthermore you should not be much concerned about tangible devotion, the experience of sweetness or tears, but rather that you should be mentally united with God within yourself by a good will in your intellect. For what pleases God above everything is a mind free from imaginations, that is images, ideas and the representations of created things. It befits a monk to be indifferent to everything created so that he can turn easily and barely to God alone within himself, be empty for him and cleave to him. For this reason deny yourself so that you can follow Christ, the Lord your God, in nakedness, who was himself poor, obedient, chaste, humble and suffering, and in whose life and death many were scandalised, as is clear from the Gospel accounts. After all, a soul which is separated from the body pays no attention to what is done to its abandoned body - whether it is burned, hanged, or reviled, and is in no way saddened by the afflictions imposed on the body, but thinks only of the Now of eternity and the One Thing which the Lord calls necessary in the Gospel. So you too should treat your body as if you were no longer in the body, but think always of the eternity of your soul in God, and direct your thoughts carefully to that One Thing of which Christ said, *For one thing is necessary.* (Luke 10.42) You will experience because of it great grace, helping you towards the acquisition of nakedness of mind and simplicity of heart. Indeed this One Thing is very much present with you if you have made yourself bare of imaginations and all other entanglements, and you will soon experience that this is so - namely when you can be empty and cleave to God with a naked and resolute mind. In this way you will remain unconquered in whatever may be inflicted on you, like the holy martyrs, fathers, the elect, and indeed all the saints who despised everything and only thought of their souls' security and eternity in God. Armed in this way within, and united to God through a good will, they spurned everything of the world as if their souls were already separated from their bodies. Consider from this how much a good will united with God is capable of, when by means of its pressing towards God the soul is effectively separated from the body in spirit and looks on its outward man as it were from a distance, and as not belonging to it. In this way it despises everything that is inflicted on itself or on its flesh as if they were happening to someone else, or not to a human being at all. For

He that is united with the Lord is one Spirit, (1 Corinthians 6.17) that is with him. So you should never dare to think or imagine anything before the Lord your God that you would blush to be heard or seen in before men, since your respect for God should be even greater than for them. It is a matter of justice in fact that all your thoughts and thinking should be raised to God alone, and the highest point of your mind should only be directed to him as if nothing existed but him, and holding to him may enjoy the perfect beginning of the life to come.

ELEVEN

HOW ONE SHOULD RESIST TEMPTATIONS AND BEAR TRIALS

Now there is no one who approaches God with a true and upright heart who is not tested by hardships and temptations. So in all these temptations see to it that even if you feel them, you do not consent to them, but bear them patiently and calmly with humility and long suffering. Even if they are blasphemies and sordid, hold firmly on to this fact in everything, that you can do nothing better or more effective against them than to consider all this sort of fantasy as a nothing. Even if they are the most vile, sordid and horrible blasphemies, simply take no notice of them, count them as nothing and despise them. Don't look on them as yours or allow yourself to make them a matter of conscience. The enemy will certainly take flight if you treat him and his company with contempt in this way. He is very proud and cannot bear to be despised and spurned. So the best remedy is to completely ignore all such temptations, like flies flying around in front of your eyes against your will. The servant of Jesus Christ must see to it that he is not so easily forced to withdraw from the face of the Lord and to be annoyed, murmur and complain over the nuisance of a single fly, that is, a trivial temptation, suspicion, sadness, distraction, need or any such adversity, when they can all be put to flight with no more than the hand of a good will directed up to God. After all, through a good will a man has God as his defender, and the holy angels as his guardians and protectors. What is more, any temptation can be overcome by a good will too, like a fly driven away from a bald head by one's hand. So *peace is for men of good will*. Indeed we can offer God nothing more valuable than a good will, since a good will in the soul is the source of all good things, and the mother of all virtues. If any one is beginning to possess that good will, he undoubtedly has what is necessary for leading a good life. For if you want what is good, but cannot do it, God will make good the deed. For it is in accordance with this eternal law that God has established with irrevocable firmness that deserts should be a matter of the will, whether in bliss or torment, reward or punishment. Love itself is a great will to serve God, a sweet desire to please God, and a fervent wish to experience God. What is more, to be tempted is not a sin, but the opportunity for exercising virtue, so that temptation can be greatly to a man's benefit, since it is held that *the whole of a man's life on earth is a testing.* (Job 7.1)

Twelve

HOW POWERFUL THE LOVE OF GOD IS

All that is said above and whatever is necessary for salvation cannot be better, more immediately and more securely achieved than by love, through which whatever is lacking of what is necessary for salvation can be made good. In love we possess the fullness of all good and the realisation of our highest longing is not denied us. After all it is love alone by which we turn back to God, are changed into God, cleave to God, and are united to God in such a way that we become one spirit with him, and are by him and through him made blessed here by grace and hereafter in glory. Now love is such that it cannot rest except in the beloved, but it does when it wins the beloved in full and peaceful possession. For love, which itself is charity, is the way of God to men and the way of man to

God. God cannot house where there is no love. So if we have love, we have God, for God is love. Furthermore nothing is sharper than love, nothing is more subtle, nothing more penetrating. It will not rest until it has by its very nature penetrated the whole power, the depth and the totality of the loved one. It wants to make itself one with the beloved, and itself, if it were possible, to be what the beloved is too. Thus it cannot bear that anything should stand between itself and the beloved object, which is God, but presses eagerly towards him. As a result it never rests until it has left everything else behind and come to him alone. For the nature of love is of a unitive and transforming power which transforms the lover into what he loves, or alternatively, makes the lover one with the other, and vice versa, in so far as is possible. This is manifest in the first place with regard to the mental powers, depending on how much the beloved is in the lover, in other words depending on how sweetly and delightfully the beloved is recalled in the mind of the lover, and in direct proportion, that is, with how much the lover strives to grasp all the things that relate to the beloved not just superficially but intimately, and to enter, as it were, into his innermost secrets. It is also manifest with regard to the emotional and affective powers when the beloved is said to be in the lover, in other words when the desire to please the beloved is found in the will and established within by the happy enjoyment of him. Alternatively, the lover is in the beloved when he is united with him by all his desire and compliance in agreement with the beloved's willing and not willing, and finds his own pleasure and pain in that of the beloved. For love draws the lover out of himself (since love is strong as death), and establishes him in the beloved, causing him to cleave closely to him. For the soul is more where it loves than where it lives, since it is in what it loves in accordance with its very nature, understanding and will, while it is in where it lives only with regard to form, which is even true for animals as well. There is nothing therefore which draws us away from the exterior senses to within ourselves, and from there to Jesus Christ and things divine, more than the love of Christ and the desire for the sweetness of Christ, for the experience, awareness and enjoyment of the presence of Christ's divinity. For there is nothing but the power of love which can lead the soul from the things of earth to the lofty summit of heaven. Nor can anyone attain the supreme beatitude unless summoned to it by love and yearning. Love after all is the life of the soul, the wedding garment and the soul's perfection, containing all the law and the prophets and our Lord's teaching. That is why Paul says to the Romans, *Love is the fulfilling of the law,* (Rom. 13.8) and in the first letter to Timothy, *The end of the commandment is love.* (1 Timothy 1.5)

THIRTEEN

THE NATURE AND VALUE OF PRAYER, AND HOW THE HEART SHOULD BE RECOLLECTED WITHIN ITSELF

Besides this, since we are incapable of ourselves for this and for any other good action whatsoever, and since we can of ourselves offer nothing to the Lord God (from whom all good things come) which is not his already, with this one exception, as he has deigned to show us both by his own blessed mouth as well as by his example, that we should turn to him in all circumstances and occasions as guilty, wretched, poor, beggarly, weak, helpless, subject servants and sons. And that we should beseech him and lay before him with complete confidence the dangers that are besetting us on all sides, completely grief-stricken in ourselves, in humble prostration of mind, in fear and love, and with recollected, composed, mature, true and naked, shamefaced affection, with great yearning and determination, and in groaning of heart and sincerity of mind. Thus we commit and offer ourselves up to him freely, securely and nakedly, fully and in everything that is ours, holding nothing back to ourselves, in such a complete and final way, that the same is fulfilled in us as in our blessed father Isaac, who speaks of this very type of prayer, saying, *Then we shall be one in God, and the Lord God will be all in all and alone in us when his own perfect love, with which he first loved us, will have become the disposition of our own hearts too.* This will come about when all our love, all our desire, all our concern, all our efforts, in fact everything we think, everything we see, speak and even hope will be God, and that unity which now is of the Father with the Son, and of the Son with the Father, will be poured into our own heart and mind as well, in such a way that just as he loves us with sincere and indissoluble love we too will be joined to him with eternal and inseparable affection. In other words we shall be united with him in such a way that whatever we hope, and whatever we say or pray will be God. This therefore should be the aim, this the concern and goal of a spiritual man - to be worthy to possess the image of future bliss in this corruptible body, and in a certain measure experience in advance how the foretaste of that heavenly bliss, eternal life and glory begins in this world. This, as I say, is the goal of all perfection, that his purified mind should be daily raised up from all bodily objects to spiritual things until all his mental activity and all his heart's desire become one unbroken prayer. So the mind must abandon the dregs of earth and press on towards to God, on whom alone should be fixed the desire of a spiritual man, for whom the least separation from that summum bonum is to be considered a living death and dreadful loss. Then, when the requisite peace has been established in his mind, when it is free from attachment to any carnal passion, and clings firmly in intention to that one supreme good, the Apostle's sayings are fulfilled, *Pray without ceasing,* (1 Thessalonians 5.17) and, *Pray in every place lifting up pure hands without anger or dispute.* (1 Timothy 2.8) For when the power of the mind is absorbed in this purity, so to speak, and is transformed from an earthly nature into the spiritual or angelic likeness, whatever it receives into itself, whatever it is occupied with, whatever it is doing, it will be pure and sincere prayer. In this way, if you continue all the time in the way we have described from the beginning, it will become as easy and clear for you to remain in contemplation in your inward and recollected state, as to live in the natural state.

FOURTEEN

THAT WE SHOULD SEEK THE VERDICT OF OUR CONSCIENCE IN EVERY DECISION

While we should strive for spiritual perfection of mind, purity and peace in God, it will be found to be not a little beneficial to this that we should return quietly into the inner secret place of the mind in the face of everything said, thought or done to us. There, withdrawn from everything else and completely recollected within ourselves, we can place ourselves in the knowledge of the truth before us and undoubtedly discover and understand that it does us absolutely no good, and rather the contrary, when we are praised or honoured by others while we recognise by the knowledge of the truth about ourselves within that we are blameworthy and guilty. And just as nothing is any help if externally people praise someone if his conscience internally accuses him, in the same way on the contrary it does a man no harm to be despised, maligned and persecuted when he remains internally just as innocent, blameless and without fault. On the contrary he has all the more good reason to rejoice in the Lord with patience, in peace and silence. After all no adversity can do any harm where evil is not in control, and just as no evil goes unpunished, so no good goes unrewarded. Nor should we wish a reward with hypocrites or expect and receive profit from men, but from the Lord God alone, not in the present, but in the future, and not in fleeting time, but in eternity. It is clear therefore that nothing is greater, and nothing better than to enter into the inner secret place of the mind always and in every tribulation and occurrence, and there to call upon the Lord Jesus Christ himself, our helper in temptations and tribulations, and to humble ourselves there by confession of sin, and praise God and Father himself, the giver of correction and the giver of consolation. Above all one should accept everything, in general and individually, in oneself or in others, agreeable or disagreeable, with a prompt and confident spirit, as coming from the hand of his infallible Providence or the order he has arranged. This attitude will lead to the forgiveness of our sins, the deliverance from bitterness, the enjoyment of joy and security, the outpouring of grace and mercy, introduction and establishment into a close relationship with God, abundant enjoyment of his presence, and firm cleaving and union with him. But let us not copy those who from hypocrisy and Pharisaism want to appear better and different from what they are, and to make a better impression and appearance before men of being something special, than they know in truth inside to be so. For it is absolute madness to seek, hunger for and aspire to human praise or renown, from oneself or others, when one is in spite of it all inwardly full of cravings and serious faults. And certainly the good things we have talked about above will flee him who chases such vanities, and he will merely bring disgrace on himself. So always keep your faults and your own incapacity before your eyes, and know yourself, so that you can be humbled and not try to avoid being held as the lowest, vilest and most abject scum by everyone when you are aware of the grave sins and serious faults in yourself. For which reason consider yourself compared to others as dross to gold, weeds to the wheat, chaff to the grain, a wolf to the sheep, Satan to the children of God. And do not seek to be respected by others and given precedence before others, but rather flee with all your heart and soul the poison of this disease, the venom of praise, the concern for boasting and vanity, lest, as the prophet says, *The wicked is praised in his own heart's desires,* (Psalm 10.4) and Isaiah, *They who speak good of you, deceive you and destroy the way of your feet,* (Isaiah 3.12) and the Lord in Luke, *Woe to you when men speak well of you!* (Luke 6.26).

FIFTEEN

HOW CONTEMPT OF HIMSELF CAN BE PRODUCED IN A MAN, AND HOW USEFUL IT IS

Furthermore the more a man recognises his own insignificance, the more he fully and the more clearly he becomes aware to the divine majesty, and the more a man is low in his own eyes for the sake of God, the truth and justice, the more precious he is in the eyes of God. For this reason let us strive with the whole strength of our desire to consider ourselves the lowest of all and to consider ourselves unworthy of any favour. We should strive to be displeasing to ourselves and pleasing only to God, while regarded as low and unworthy of consideration by others. Above all not to be moved by difficulties, afflictions and insults, and not to be upset by those who inflict such things on us, or entertain evil thoughts against them or be indignant, but to believe steadfastly and with equanimity in all insults, slights, blows and dereliction that it is only appropriate. For in truth he who is really penitent and grieving before God hates to be honoured and loved by all, and does not try to manipulate things so as to avoid being to some degree hated, neglected and despised right to the end, so that he can be truly humbled and sincerely cleave to God alone with a pure heart. Indeed, for loving God alone and hating oneself more than anything, and desiring to be despised by others we do not require external work or physical strength, but rather physical solitude, the labour of the heart, and peace of mind so that, as it were, by labour of the heart and the disposition of the inmost mind, one may rise up, casting off from oneself lower and physical things, and so soar up, ascending to things heavenly and divine. For indeed in so doing we are changed into God, and this will especially take place when without judgement, condemnation or contempt of our neighbour, we choose rather to be considered as scum and a disgrace by everyone and to be despised as unclean filth by everyone than to experience all sorts of different delicacies or to be honoured and exalted by men, or enjoy all sorts of transitory physical forms of well-being and comfort. We should not desire any pleasure of this present, mortal and physical life but rather to mourn, bewail and lament our offences, faults and sins without ceasing, and to perfectly despise and annihilate ourselves, and from day to day to be considered more and more abject by others, while in all our insignificance we become worthless even in our own eyes, so that we can be pleasing to God alone, love him alone, and cleave to him alone. We should not wish to be concerned about anything except the Lord Jesus Christ himself who alone should reside in our affections, and we should not be concerned or anxious about anything except him on whose dominion and providence everything in general and individually depends. So from now on it should not be your aim to seek enjoyment but to truly mourn with all your heart. For that reason, if you do not mourn, mourn for that, while if you do mourn, mourn especially that you have brought the cause of your pain on yourself by your own great offences and infinite sins. For just as a condemned man on receiving his sentence does not concern himself about the seating of the spectators, so he who laments and is genuinely mourning is not interested in pleasures, resentment, fame or wrongs or things of that sort. And just as townsfolk and contemned criminals have different accommodation, the state and position of those who are mourning and have committed offences deserving punishment ought to be completely different from those who are innocent and under no obligation. Otherwise there would be no difference between the guilty and the innocent in matters of punishment and reward. The result would be great dereliction of duty, and evil behaviour would have more freedom than goodness. So everything must be renounced, everything despised, everything rejected and avoided, so that we can lay a firm foundation of penitent grieving. Then, loving Jesus Christ in reality, yearning for him, and holding him in one's heart, in reality experiencing pain for one's sins and faults, in reality seeking to know the coming Kingdom, while with true faith bearing in mind the reality of the torments and eternal judgement, and firmly and fully taking up the recollection and fear of one's own death, we should be aware of nothing else, and not care or be worried about anything else. For that reason, he who hurries towards the blessed state of impassibility and towards God should reckon himself to have experienced great loss every day that he is not insulted and despised. Impassibility after all is freedom from vices and passions and purity of heart and the adornment of all virtues. So consider yourself as already dead since there is no doubt that you have got to die. And as a final thought let this be the test for you of whether any thought, word or action of yours is of God, whether you are made more humble because of it, more inward and more recollected and established in God. If you find it is otherwise in yourself, you should be suspicious about it, whether it be not according to God, unacceptable to you and not to your benefit.

SIXTEEN

HOW GOD'S PROVIDENCE INCLUDES EVERYTHING

Certainly if we are to come directly, safely and nakedly to our Lord God without hindrance, freely and peacefully, as explained above, and be securely joined to him with even mind in prosperity or adversity, whether in life or in death, then our job is to commit everything unhesitatingly and resolutely, in general and individually, to his unquestionable and infallible providence. This is hardly surprising since it is he alone who gives to all things their being, their capacity and their action - that is, their strength, operation, nature, manner and order in number, weight and measure. Especially since just as a work of art presupposes a prior operation of nature, in the same way the operation of nature presupposes the work of God, creating, sustaining, ordering and administering it, for to him alone belong infinite power, wisdom, goodness and inherent mercy, justice, truth, love, and unchanging timelessness and omnipresence. So nothing can exist or act by its own power unless it acts in the power of God himself, who is the prime mover and the first principle, who is the cause of every action, and the actor in every agent. For so far as the nature of the order of things is concerned, God provides for everything without intermediary right down to the last detail. So nothing, from the greatest to the smallest things, can escape God's eternal providence, or fall away from it, whether in matters of the will, of causal events, or even of accidental circumstances outside of one's control. But God cannot do anything which does not fall under the order of his own providence, just as he cannot do anything which is not subject to its operation. Divine providence therefore extends to everything, in general and in particular, even including a man's thoughts. On which subject Scripture has this to say, *Cast all your worries upon him, for he takes care of you.* (1 Peter 5.7) And again the prophet says, *Cast your care upon the Lord, and he will feed you.* (Psalm 55.22) *And, Look at the nations of men, my son, and see that no one ever put his trust in the Lord, and was disappointed. For who has been faithful to his commandments and been abandoned?* (Sirach 2.22) And our Lord himself said, *Do not be anxious, saying, What shall we eat?* (Matthew 6.25) So whatever and however much we can hope from God, we shall undoubtedly receive, as Deuteronomy says, *Every place where you feet tread shall be yours.* (Deuteronomy 11.24) For a man shall receive all that he is able to desire, and so far as he can reach with his foot of faith, even so much shall he possess. That is why Bernard says, "God, the maker of everything is so abounding in mercy that whatever size grace cup of faith we are able to hold out to him, we shall undoubtedly have it filled." And so Mark has it, *All that you ask in prayer believing that you will receive it, will be given you.* (Mark 11.24) So the stronger and the more vehement our faith in God is, and the more reverently and persistently it is offered up to God, the more surely, the more abundantly and the quicker what we hoped for will be accomplished and obtained. Indeed if in doing this our faith in God is weak and slow to rise to God on account of the multitude and magnitude of our sins, we should remember this, that everything is possible with God, and that what he wishes is bound to take place, while what he does not wish cannot possibly happen, and that it is as easy for him to forgive and cancel countless sins, however enormous, as to do it with a single sin. While a sinner cannot, of himself, rise from innumerable sins, and free and absolve himself from them, and not even from just one sin. For we are unable not only to do, but even to think anything good, of ourselves, but this is from God. Nonetheless it is much more dangerous, other things being equal, to be ensnared in many sins than in a single one, since no sin is left unpunished, and every mortal sin deserves infinite punishment, and this by the rigour of justice since any such sin is against God who is indeed worthy of infinite reverence, dignity and honour. What is more, according to the Apostle Paul, *God knows his own* (2 Timothy 2.19), and it is impossible for any of them to perish by the whirlwinds and floods of any error, scandal, schism, persecution, heresy, tribulation, adversity or temptation, for he has foreseen from eternity and unchangeably the number of his elect and the extent of their merits in such a way that everything good and bad, what is theirs and not theirs, prosperity and adversity, all work together for them for good, except indeed that they appear even more glorious and commendable in adversity. So let us commit everything with full assurance, in general and in particular, confidently and unhesitatingly to divine providence, by which God permits however much and whatever sort of evil to happen to us. For it is good and will lead to good, since he permits it to exist, and it would not exist unless he permitted it to exist. Nor could it exist otherwise or more than he permits it to, because he knows how to, has the power to, and wills to change and convert it into something better. For just as it is by operation of providence that all good things exist, so it is by its permission that all bad things are changed into good. In this way in fact God's power, wisdom and mercy are shown forth through Christ our redeemer - his mercy and his justice, the power of grace and the weakness of nature, the beauty of everything in the association of opposites, the approval of the good, and the malice and punishment of the wicked. Similarly the contrition of the converted sinner, his confession, and penitence, the kindness of God, piety, charity and his praise and goodness (all show forth God's power and wisdom). Yet it does not always lead to good in those who do ill, but, as is usually the case, to great danger and extreme evil, in the loss, that is, of grace and their place in glory, and in the incurring of guilt and punishment, sometimes even eternal punishment, from which may Jesus Christ defend us. Amen.

INDEX OF SCRIPTURE REFERENCES

Deuteronomy

11:24

Job

7:1

Psalms

10:4   16:8   17:15   55:22   55:22   73:28

Song of Solomon

3:4

Isaiah

3:12

Matthew

6:6   6:25

Mark

11:24

Luke

6:26   10:42   17:21

John

17:3

Romans

13:8

1 Corinthians

6:17   15:46

Philippians

4:6

1 Thessalonians

5:17

1 Timothy

1:5   2:8

2 Timothy

2:19

1 Peter

5:7   5:7

Wisdom of Solomon

7:11

Sirach

2:22

www.ingramcontent.com/pod-product-compliance
Lightning Source LLC
Chambersburg PA
CBHW020522030426
42337CB00011B/517